September 11 AND YOU

September 11 AND YOU

TARGUM/FELDHEIM

First published 2004
Copyright © 2004 by Moshe Goldberger
P.O. Box 82
Staten Island, NY 10309
718-948-2548
ISBN 1-56871-318-5

Published by:
TARGUM PRESS, INC.
22700 W. Eleven Mile Rd.
Southfield, MI 48034
E-mail: targum@netvision.net.il
Fax: 888-298-9992
www.targum.com

Distributed by:
FELDHEIM PUBLISHERS
202 Airport Executive Park
Nanuet, NY 10954

Printing plates, "Frank," Jerusalem

Printed in Israel

With thanks to:

Rabbi Eliezer Gevirtz
Rabbi Menachem Goldman
Rabbi Mordechai Gelber
Yitzchok E. Gold
Binyamin Siegel
Charles S. Mamiye
Bob Burg
Daniel Bock
Daniel Lemberg
David Goldberger
Mordechai Kairey
Dr. J. Cohen
Zissel Leib Colmar
and others

Contents

Preface

On the morning of Tuesday, September 11, 2001 (5761), two commercial airplanes were hijacked by terrorists and crashed into the World Trade Center Twin Towers in New York City. Both office buildings collapsed within a short time. About 2,800 lives were lost. (Two additional commercial airplanes were also hijacked that day, one of them crashing into the Pentagon, with a loss of another two hundred lives.) There was no advance warning of this attack, which is now known as "September 11."

This shocking event has served as a wake-up call to the American public — and the entire world. Much new legislation was passed. The United States is currently engaged in two wars, in various stages. The event was, without a doubt, a significant event in recent American history.

It is now almost three years later. For some, September 11 is starting to fade from our memories.

If you lived during the era of September 11, or you are hearing about it now, there are definite messages that Hashem intends for your benefit, messages not limited by time. We do not believe that anything in life occurs randomly. Certainly, such a catastrophic event has significant lessons for all of us. We have to utilize the lessons to be learned from this event in deciding how to direct our lives.

Let me confess that this book is partly directed toward myself and my family. What is Hashem's message to me and to others? The answers are based on timeless Torah teachings of our Sages.

We all have inner resources that need to be stimulated, utilized, and developed. We need to set goals, zero in on them, and make them happen, with Hashem's help. We need to learn the Torah's response to every event, internalize it, and implement the lessons learned with logic, determination, ambition, and prayer.

September 11 was a shocking event — an event that has far-reaching ramifications at every level. However, it is also a source of inspiration that will open our hearts and minds to expand to the levels Hashem expects of us.

The question "What is it that Hashem is asking of us?" (*Devarim* 10:12) should be ringing in our ears, and we should be dedicating our lives to responding to it.

Chapter 1

How to Choose

Choose life!
(*Devarim* 30:19)

You have the potential to have a good life. You have it within you, and, by your actions, you can deserve it. Hashem wants it for you: He engineered you with the capacity to achieve it. There is no one else exactly like you in history. Hashem made the world with you in mind and He has instructed you to say regularly with conviction: "The world was created because of me!" (*Sanhedrin* 37a).

You were given opportunities that you can choose to take advantage of to accomplish your greatest dreams. The limits on what you can achieve are mainly those you place on yourself, by your choices.

If I am not for myself, who will be for me?
(*Avos* 1:14)

Just as some people chose the path of wickedness

to topple the Twin Towers, you, *lehavdil*, can choose to build new buildings or achieve other positive accomplishments, with Hashem's help. You may say to this, "Who are you kidding?" "I'm stuck; I can't get out of the rut I am in." "I'm just not capable of great things — I am barely able to make a living." You may be laughing at this whole idea.

We all have such doubts and fears.

This is part of the challenge of life. We think that we are lacking skills, education, "connections," and so on. We sometimes feel lost. With Hashem's help, we can learn how to extricate ourselves from these feelings. We have unlimited resources and opportunities in our grasp. We can learn how to acquire and implement Torah guidelines that will help us achieve our goals.

You can change your life!

You can choose life!

*   *   *

Pirkei Avos sums up the key principle to achieving success in life in three Hebrew words (four in English): "*Hu hayah omer* — He used to say." The incredible power of choice that Hashem implanted in you has to be activated by determination and repetition. The preface to *Mesilas Yesharim* teaches that when one regularly reviews a goal, it will become part of him. You can train yourself to be happier, more alert, more confident, and more positive.

If you are thinking that this won't work for you or that you have tried self-help programs in the past and were unsuccessful, realize that you have chosen to accept these negative thoughts. You must replace these ideas with: "Let me modify my thinking and learn to internalize this Torah approach." You can learn to control your mind. You can choose to build towers of your own and demolish wickedness.

You have nothing to lose and everything to gain. This program is free and invigorating. You do not need to purchase expensive equipment or building materials. However, there is a unique, priceless component to this endeavor: you!! You need to commit yourself to what we will be describing with zest and determination. Yes, hard work is required, as the Mishnah teaches: "According to the difficulty is the reward" (*Avos* 5:27).

You can choose to focus on being happy and having positive thoughts. You can choose to love Hashem, love people, love Torah, and love mitzvos. You can keep your mind clearly focused on what you desire and refrain from thinking about failure. Hashem can help you achieve everything you need, but you must be truly ready for it.

If you decide to plant a seed and care for it, Hashem will generally make it grow. We can learn from those who think properly, our Torah Sages, how to think more effectively, to plant the right seeds, to nurture them, and to reap the terrific results.

You can choose right now to live by the motto of "A good mind will always be happy" (*Mishlei* 15:15) and change your life in that direction. You may have $100,000 in the bank or $50, it doesn't make a difference — because your happiness is dependent on your attitude, not on how much you have (see *Avos* 4:1).

September 11 and you: September 11, 2001, was a week before Rosh HaShanah that year. The tragic attacks were the subject of many sermons on that Rosh Hashanah and Yom Kippur.

Nearly everyone approaches the *Yamim Nora'im* ("Days of Awe," i.e., Rosh HaShanah and Yom Kippur) with special feelings. It is a time of introspection in preparation for Hashem's annual review and judgment of our lives. It is a time of making plans for the year to follow and a time to pray for a year of health, happiness, and good tidings.

Was it a coincidence that September 11 occurred a week before Rosh HaShanah? Obviously not.

Every day is the beginning of a new time period for us and everyone in our lives. Do not let the effect of "9/11" fade from your memory. Do not wait until next Rosh HaShanah. Make a choice now to develop a personalized growth program for a new and happier life.

"Choose life!"

Chapter 2

Change Your Pictures

Look at three things and you will not come to sin:
Know what is above you — an eye that sees, an
ear that hears, and all your deeds are recorded.
(Avos 2:1)

This Mishnah is teaching us that nothing we do, whether good or bad, will be overlooked. We need to imagine a great video camera always filming us. Realize that everything you do makes a difference.

"Do not consider yourself wicked" (*Avos* 2:18). You have to realize that you are a significant individual. You are important, valuable, loved by others, and loved by Hashem. This should motivate you to be more positive, determined, and ambitious.

The way you think about something makes a great difference. Thus it is very important to study the Torah outlook on every aspect of life.

Before the shocking change in Manhattan's skyline, we could not imagine the skyline looking any different. But now we realize that things can change drastically (even in a moment!). Similarly, we can make solid improvements in our lives by changing our focus and direction and striving for new goals in a steadfast, determined manner.

The Mishnah mentioned above — "Do not consider yourself wicked" — also teaches two other important lessons:

1. Be careful with how you say the Shema.

2. Pray in a heartfelt manner for Hashem's mercy.

How does one change his self-perspective from negative to positive?

The Talmud (*Kiddushin* 49b) teaches that a person can become righteous in one moment by means of thoughts of *teshuvah*. You can change your values, beliefs, and performance in any area of life by rethinking your self-image. Look closer at this word — *self-image* — for it also contains the root of the word *imagine*.

Imagine that your potential is unlimited.

Imagine that you say Shema with much more focus and concentration and completely accept Hashem as your King. Imagine praying directly to Hashem and pleading for more assistance in all areas of life.

Imagine asking Hashem for a raise so that you can pay all of your bills.

Imagine that you are more calm, confident, and determined.

Imagine that you can set goals and achieve all the important things you want to accomplish.

Imagine....

What is the key method for achieving all these positive pictures? One of the Sages of the Mishnah, Rabbi Shimon, spelled it out when he was asked: "What is the best approach for success in life?" (*Avos* 2:13). His answer is: "One who visualizes the future" (ibid.).

Your vision of yourself and your future accomplishments can make all the difference. The values, qualities, and ideals you seek will guide and shape your behavior. But first you need to clarify them to yourself visually.

It is essential to like and respect oneself in a realistic, yet idealistic, manner. Develop a clear, positive, exciting, and inspiring picture of yourself achieving the goals you are seeking, with Hashem's help. Think about becoming your very best by performing at maximum capacity.

We need to keep reviewing the basics of life from *Chumash Bereishis*. Hashem created you in His image with the intellectual ability to achieve incredible greatness. Hashem declares that everything He created (including you) is very good (*Bereishis* 1:31)! You have the potential to excel in life. You can develop yourself, treat others properly, bounce back up if you fall down, and succeed on all fronts, with Hashem's help.

But there are also challenges that Hashem sends along our path. We must be aware of giving up in the face of failure and setting self-limitations. "A person's foolishness can corrupt his path, but in his heart he blames Hashem" (*Mishlei* 19:3).

If you keep on thinking, "I'm not good enough," you will short-circuit your ambition. You need to tell yourself instead, "I may not be as good as I want to be, but that's not the way it needs to be! I see myself changing rapidly, with Hashem's help." Hashem can help you excel in any area in which you are determined to develop your potential.

Hillel, the famous Sage, would always say to himself: "If I am not for myself, who will be for me?" (*Avos* 1:14). Thus, he was saying, "I can do it!" Positive self-talk is the method to implant proper Torah attitudes in our minds and hearts.

September 11 and you: Even the downs in life are not discouragements when we view them as all part of Hashem's process to help us achieve success. "All that the Merciful One does is for good" (*Berachos* 60b). Every setback is sent to teach us important lessons. Even a super tragedy like the downing of the Twin Towers can wake us up and give us a charge to become unstoppable in our growth.

"A righteous person falls seven times, and he keeps getting up" (*Mishlei* 24:16). Even if you have failed to accomplish your desired goal many times, if your goal has meaning to you, do not give up, but "get up" to pursue success with Hashem's help.

Hashem is watching us and guiding us. We need to upgrade our view of ourselves and then we will grow more in positive steps.

Chapter 3

Seeing Good

*Who is the man who desires life, who loves days
to see good?*
(*Tehillim* 34:13)

The key to this phrase is at the end of the verse:
the desire "to *see* good."

We need to develop a cheerful outlook and
happy expectations. They make a great difference.
"A good mind is always at a party" (*Mishlei* 15:15).

The more optimistic your attitude is, the happier
you will be.

Tehillim 34 continues: "Turn away from the negative and do good...."

You can eliminate negative thoughts and think
positive ones, thus generating feelings of happiness
and fulfillment.

We can think of the destruction of the Twin
Towers and feel weak, angry, frustrated, and unhappy. Or we can think about how we can utilize
that event to grow, to rebuild, to encourage, and to

empower.... Imagine if, as a result of the destruction of the Twin Towers, we stumble upon a discovery that saves 50,000 lives. Would your thoughts about that event change — at least, to some degree?

The Talmud (*Yoma* 86b) teaches an amazing concept: The way we repent for our past misdeeds makes all the difference in whether they are held against us or they become merits on our behalf. The more we regret misdeeds and wish we had done the right thing, the greater is Hashem's forgiveness. Thus, it is never too late to redo our past! You can turn a past event into a positive one by rethinking it now.

Avos 2:13 outlines five pathways to achieving success: (1) a good eye, (2) a good friend, (3) a good neighbor, (4) one who foresees the consequences of his actions, and (5) a good heart.

The Sages explain "a good eye" as seeing things in a positive light. When things do not go as you had hoped, instead of blowing up with anger and resentment, learn to view the situation in a positive way.

One of the best areas to apply this concept is with our dealings with other people, who sometimes seem to be inconsiderate. You can keep rehashing a hurtful situation and judging the other person harshly, or you can apply the principle in *Avos* (1:6): "Judge people in a meritorious way." Use your intelligence and your imagination to find excuses for someone's negative behavior. For example, maybe he wasn't feeling well. Why be upset or resentful if it will only cause you harm?

When you are optimistic, you see more possibilities and opportunities, and as a result you are happier and more effective. You see solutions to problems; you are hopeful and caring. When you look back at 9/11, you can see the people who were saved and all the good people who helped and all those who tried to help.

Forgiveness

Included in the concept of the good eye is the idea of forgiving others who may have hurt you in some way. How so? When you refuse to forgive others, your vision becomes blurred and you cannot evaluate others properly; your vision is tinted by the resentment you harbor. If you forgive others, our Sages teach, Hashem will forgive you (*Rosh HaShanah* 17a). This is based on Hashem's system of dealing with us measure for measure (*middah keneged middah*).

But what is wrong with not forgiving others in the first place?

If we refuse to forgive others, we are not being like Hashem, who is "good to all" and merciful to all of His creations (*Tehillim* 145:9). Every time we pray the weekday *Shemoneh Esrei* we ask Hashem to forgive us, and we say: "For You are the Merciful One who abundantly forgives." This forgiveness from

Hashem teaches us to do the same for others.

By forgiving others, we free ourselves from pettiness and negative emotions.

Imagine your attitude toward life if you were like Aharon, who loved everyone and pursued peace (*Avos* 1:12). You would always be optimistic, cheerful, enthusiastic, friendly, and calm. In contrast, refusal to forgive leaves you angry, stressful, anxious, and unhappy. Why do that to yourself?

We have Torah guidelines for when to forgive and when not to. For example, you should forgive your parents for all the wrong things you might think they have done to you: You owe them so much for bringing you into this world that the Torah obligates you to honor and respect them forever. Imagine if someone gave you a gift of ten million dollars and subsequently stepped on your toe by mistake. Would you complain? Be happy and grateful that you are alive and forgive your parents for anything else.

The Rambam (*Hilchos Dei'os*, ch. 6) outlines the procedure for the mitzvah of forgiving others. He teaches that you should not hate a person in your heart, but you should privately ask him or her outright, "Why did you do such and such to me?" It also works the other way. If you hurt someone, go and apologize. Say, "I'm very sorry for.... Please forgive me."

The exception to these halachos are people who choose total wickedness. People such as Amalek who choose evil are to be destroyed (see *Devarim* 25:17–19). "Those who love Hashem hate evil" (*Tehillim* 97:10). By eradicating such evil, we are saving lives, promoting peace, and fulfilling the Torah precept to "destroy evil from your midst."

Not only must we forgive others, but we also have to forgive ourselves when we do *aveiros*. We must repent for our wickedness and insensitivity, but then we must realize how much Hashem loves and cherishes those who repent (Rambam, *Hilchos Teshuvah* 7:4). With proper regret, we can change the past.

Whenever you think of some past mistake you've made, say, "I regret what I did. Hashem, please forgive me."

September 11 and you: You can look back at a negative experience and find something good, a reinterpretation that can make all the difference. You can learn how to utilize the event to become a better and wiser person. We are doing that right now in using the tragic events of 9/11 to reevaluate what is important in life.

Chapter 4

Expand Your Horizons

Y ou have the power to achieve health, wealth, friends, peace, completeness — whatever you really desire, with Hashem's help. "Open your mouth wide, and I will fill it" (*Tehillim* 81:11). Why limit yourself to half a piece of bread when you can have a whole piece?

The above verse from *Tehillim* begins with: "I am Hashem, your God, who took you out of the land of Egypt." Did the Jews in Egypt dream of leaving that land after having been enslaved for 210 years? Surely they dreamt about leaving Egypt but thought that actually leaving was impossible. Yet Hashem made it happen. So, too, we need to dream big and bigger, and we must dream with expectations that our dreams are not merely dreams — Hashem can make them real. Hashem's greatness is unlimited. When we work with Him, we cannot be satisfied with small dreams.

We need to dream of rebuilding the Twin Towers,

at least ten more of them, with Hashem's help. We also need more learning programs in these new towers — all over the world, maybe even a yeshivah in each tower. Every business should have a central conference room where there are daily minyanim and Torah classes. Every businessperson should have a place where he can seclude himself during break times for Torah study.

Achieving success is a long, arduous process. However, don't limit your thinking. Don't worry excessively about your chances of failure. Be excited, for Hashem encourages you to think big and ask for His assistance.

Why does the verse from *Tehillim* instruct us to "open our mouths wide"? Why not just to think big or increase our desires? We need to visualize our goals with vivid clarity and to make them tangible. Taste them as if they are "in your mouth." Pray to Hashem "with your mouth" with true sincerity. When, after 120 years, you will come before the Heavenly Throne and you are asked to give an accounting, will you be able to say that you opened your mouth wide to ask Hashem for assistance in reaching your goals when you had a chance to do so?

To create your ideal future vision you need to imagine that you have no limits. Pretend that you have all the time, money, connections, resources, opportunities, and help that you need. Imagine an ideal situation in every respect.

What great goal would you choose if you had a guarantee that you would succeed? Where would you like to work? What would you like to do? When David HaMelech expresses his great goal in life, he says: "One thing I have asked of Hashem, that is what I seek, to dwell in the house of Hashem all the days of my life..." (*Tehillim* 27:4). Is David being repetitive here with his statement "one thing have I asked of Hashem, that is what I seek"? We can explain that he begins with a vision of an ideal future, but then he focuses on turning his dream into concrete, practical goals.

What practical steps can we take to achieve our goals? Try using the following seven-step approach that is based on our Sages' teaching, in seven (Hebrew) words: "*Baderech she'adam rotzeh leileich, bah molichin oso* — On the path one is determined to go, on it [Hashem] will lead him" (*Makos* 10b):

1. *Baderech* — on the path: What specific path are you seeking? It is essential to focus on clear goals in order to succeed in achieving them. Ask yourself, "What do I really, really want?" When you know what you desire, you will stop wasting so much time.

2. *Adam* — a person: Put all of yourself into the program. You must use all of your faculties,

your common sense, your communication skills — everything you have. Are you willing to go through all it will take to get to your destination? Or are you looking for some shortcut? Hashem deals with us measure for measure, *middah keneged middah*. Thus, if you cut corners on your path to success, He may not provide you with full assistance. Are you willing to do whatever it takes in order to reap the benefits?

3. *Rotzeh* — determined: Strengthen your commitment by putting it in writing. Why is every Jew commanded to write for himself a *sefer Torah* (Torah scroll) [*Devarim* 31:19]? Why is a Jewish king obligated to write two *sifrei Torah* (Torah scrolls) for himself? [ibid. 17:18]? Writing intensifies the lesson and deepens one's commitment. As you write your goals you will increase your resolve to do whatever is necessary to achieve them.

   The Talmud teaches: "Fortunate is one who comes here [the next world] with his learning in his hand" (*Bava Basra* 10b). The Maharsha says that this alludes to putting our learning in writing, for that helps make it a part of you.

4. *Leileich* — to go: Take action. You cannot lie in bed and wish for your goals to come running after you. Opportunity will not knock on your

door if you are not running on the path towards it. You must make an effort —
hishtadlus. To succeed in meeting your goals,
you may have to start each day a bit earlier
and work a bit harder than you are accus-
tomed to. You may have to upgrade your
skills and knowledge. But if you do nothing,
you will never get anywhere. "According to
the difficulty is the reward" (*Avos* 5:27).

5. *Bah* — in it: Analyze your pathway. You
should have a general outline of the vision
for your goal, but you also need a step-by-
step plan of action. Perhaps make a written
checklist to ensure that you get everything
done.

6. *Molichin* — [Hashem] will lead: Pray and pray
some more. Putting your key in the ignition is
not guaranteed to turn the car on. You have
to pray that Hashem assists you in bringing
your goal to fruition. Each step of the way requires additional prayers to the Source of all.
"Hope to Hashem, strengthen yourself...and
hope to Hashem" (*Tehillim* 27:14). The Talmud (*Berachos* 32b) explains that this means
to pray again and again.

7. *Oso* — him: Stick with your program and
keep advancing every day. Hashem will not
lead you to where you want to go if you do
not continue with your own efforts. You are

the main player here. Take a step forward in the direction of your goal every day. The more you dwell on it, the more you demonstrate and develop your desire to make it happen. Your actions show you are serious about your goal.

When you are totally committed, Hashem is also "committed" to helping you. Sometimes we even discover unusual surprises occurring to help things work out right. Unexpected resources, unforeseen incidents, and material assistance seem to click in when we push forward with total dedication.

September 11 and you: The original Twin Towers are no longer in existence. However, as we write this book, plans are being made for new structures that will fill the void. In addition, all over the world, lessons have been learned and are being learned from this terrible tragedy.

A person must continue to move forward. Stagnation is not an option.

Chapter 5

Wealth Ambitions

What can a person do to become wealthy?... He should engage in business and carry out his business dealings with faithfulness...and pray to [Hashem,] the Owner of all wealth.
(Niddah 70b)

Why does the Talmud spend time on the subject of how to become wealthy? We need to clarify the Torah's view on material bounty. Rav Simchah Zissel (the Alter of Kelm) explains, based on *Bereishis* 15:13–14, that the Torah views wealth positively. When Hashem informs Avraham Avinu of the future of his descendants, He says, "Know that your descendants will be enslaved in a strange land...but they will leave [it] with great wealth." From this we see that wealth is a benefit that would make Avraham Avinu rejoice.

Wealth is one of the blessings Hashem bestows on those whom He favors. This explains why the Torah and our Sages make a point of mentioning that all three of our forefathers, Avraham, Yitzchak, and Yaakov, became very wealthy individuals. Likewise, Moshe Rabbeinu, Yosef HaTzaddik, and all of the prophets were wealthy people (*Nedarim* 38a).

It is essential that we learn the Torah system for achieving wealth and why it is a positive, noteworthy endeavor.

How to Achieve Wealth

The main two ingredients to achieving wealth, as the *gemara* quoted above teaches, are to engage in business with the right attitude of faith in Hashem and to pray to Hashem, the Owner of all wealth. Thus, we learn that one must do his part, i.e., he must engage in some type of occupation or business, and he needs to pray for Hashem's help. "If I am not for myself, who will be for me?" (*Avos* 1:14). Hard work is part of the equation.

Mishlei (10:4) states openly: "The hand of the diligent will become wealthy."

On a simple level, this means not wasting time at work. Idle socializing with coworkers or on the phone is not justified. Starting late, taking long breaks, and leaving early are forms of theft that hurt the employer (or company) and the employee. We learn from Yaakov Avinu that one should work with total dedication to his boss, even when the boss is far from righteous. Although Yaakov's boss was his father-in-law, Lavan, the father of Rachel and Leah, he was an unfair person who took advantage of Yaakov many times. Hashem rewarded Yaakov with great wealth for his honesty. The Rambam points out, at the conclusion of the laws of employment (*Hilchos Sechirus* 13:13) that Yaakov's dedication to his work, in the face of these very difficult challenges, serves as an example of success in the workplace and the rewards that follow.

The Rambam (ibid.) sums up two rules for an employee:

1. He may not steal from his employer by wasting a little time here and a little time there. He must be careful with his employer's time.

2. He must work with all of his strength (including the mental exertion necessary to achieve the best results), as did Yaakov (see *Bereishis* 31:6).

If you associate with and befriend those employees in your workplace who waste time and do not invest all of their energy into their work, and you are influenced by them, although you may keep your job, you will not merit the blessings that accrue to those who are careful to fulfill the Torah's guidelines for proper behavior.

Work is not something one does only when the boss is watching. Work is a Torah value. We need to use our time well because Hashem is always watching us. Consider framing the words of the Rambam above and keeping a copy at your workplace for a constant reminder. (You can contact us at P.O. Box 82, Staten Island, NY, 10309 for reminder cards.) The Mishnah (*Avos* 1:10) teaches us, "Love work" — do it sincerely, seriously, and wholeheartedly.

"Love" also means to make work fun. To be successful at any profession or job, we need to be positive, flexible, and agreeable. But the focus has to be on accomplishing the work efficiently and successfully.

From the Rambam, we learned that we must not waste time and we should work hard. Yet another important point can be learned from Yaakov Avinu's statement, "With all my strength I served [Lavan]" (*Bereishis* 31:6). By working very hard, Yaakov succeeded in satisfying Lavan, a fact that can be derived from Lavan's schemes to keep Yaakov working for him indefinitely. In fact, Yaakov worked for Lavon for twenty years (ibid., 38).

If one is lazy at the workplace, besides stealing from his boss in the halachic sense, he is also stealing from his own potential. *Pirkei Avos* teaches that Hashem is the Great Employer and He wants us to develop a sense of urgency to accomplish mitzvos in our daily lives (*Avos* 2:19–20). We need to develop the habits of speed and efficiency. The *Mesilas Yesharim* says that righteous people do everything with swiftness. However, one should beware of act-ing hastily or finishing a job just to say that he's finished. Accuracy is part of the desired goal.

Ask yourself now:

- How can I add more value to my work today?

- How can I focus all of my energy on my job while at work today?

- Which part of my job is most valuable and how can I do it more?

Improving Our Prayer

The second key to wealth, mentioned at the beginning of this chapter, is prayer. There are many ways we can improve our prayer, even with small steps. You may not be thinking of joining a *vasikin* (early morning) minyan at this point, but you can surely learn from the concept. The Talmud (*Berachos* 9b) teaches that those who pray at the crack of dawn will be successful all day long. Davening early in the morning shows a person's attitude and personality. It demonstrates his desire to connect with Hashem, his Creator, and to fulfill His will as soon as possible. You can get more done in the morning, clear your mind, plan your day, and get to work fully energized.

The Talmud (*Berachos* 31b) also teaches that the great righteous Sages would always prepare for an hour before prayers and then stay on for an hour afterwards. We should get into the habit of always being on time to minyan. When this habit becomes ingrained in us, we can go on to the next step — being early.

Staying after the prayers are over, even for only a few more minutes, is worthwhile, too. You have time to wrap up your inspired thoughts and to plan your day.

When the Twin Towers fell, there were many people who, for various reasons, were not there that morning. Some had the good fortune of being "delayed" because of their morning prayers. The word "delayed" is really not the right one. In fact, looking at prayer as an activity that delays one from reaching his desired activities is surely an attitude that needs to be changed. When we have an opportunity to pray to Hashem, which happens at least three times a day, we are meeting with the Creator and Controller of the universe, the Owner of all wealth, the Source of everything. We need to respect these times and realize how precious they are.

To sum up: We began with the concept of wealth and how the *avos*, our forefathers, were rewarded for their diligence with great wealth. We then discussed the work ethic according to halachah as taught by the Rambam. We further discussed the benefits of being an early riser.

Before leaving this topic, we want to stress that

being on time and doing a great job is the way to live. However, we don't want to give the impression that a person should spend all his time working and that there is nothing as important as work. Rather, we want to stress the importance and rewards of being a worker who is guided by Torah principles, for in the end, a person's annual livelihood is established on Rosh HaShanah (*Beitzah* 16a). An overemphasis on work will not increase the income decreed for you. If there is no sustenance, there can be no Torah (*Avos* 3:21). It is also true that if there is no Torah, there is no sustenance (ibid.). We need a proper balance.

September 11 and you: It was widely reported that after the two jet airliners crashed into the Twin Towers, the people in the towers who knew they were trapped sought to communicate with their loved ones. We also know that the passengers in the two additional hijacked planes sought to communicate with their loved ones before those planes crashed.

"Who is wealthy? One who rejoices with his portion" (*Avos* 4:1). These people, who were in mortal danger, were focusing on what life is about. They were not concerned about earning more money. They were concerned about their loved ones and about saying their final prayers.

Rav Avigdor Miller, *zt"l*, would constantly stress that a person must be happy that he is alive and thank Hashem for what he has. We must always strive to not only rejoice with our lot but also to realize how many blessings we have. We express our appreciation to Hashem daily for our eyes, our clothes, our ability to walk, and so on. While it is important to earn money, one must never lose sight of what is really important and cherish it.

Chapter 6

Learning More

To excel in life, we need to devote ourselves to learning more. Learning Torah is, of course, the most important application of this concept. However, we can also improve our lives, our relationships with others, and our work performance if we develop the learning habit.

> *Who is wise? One who learns from every person.*
> (*Avos* 4:1)

This *mishnah* can help us accomplish every goal we set for ourselves. Perhaps there are people you know who seem to be doing better than you at their jobs. Can you do anything about it? Yes! You can observe them to see what you can learn from what they do. If it seems appropriate, you can even ask someone how he is so successful or if he has any recommendations for you. Rather than be envious, you can learn from the people who are doing better than you.

When the *mishnah* says that a wise person learns from everyone, this even includes our enemies. When the terrorists decided to destroy the Twin Towers, they came up with the idea of using simple and common tools to cause mass destruction. *Lehavdil* (in contrast), we can learn a powerful lesson from this: to use any tools at our disposal to improve ourselves, even those that seem very simple.

What Can We Learn?

In achieving our goals in life, we must realize that we can learn anything we need to in order to achieve the goals we set for ourselves.

Perhaps you would like to

- lose weight,

- get a better job,

- improve your marriage,

- improve your parenting skills, or

- increase your learning skills,

but you feel that you can't. This is false — if you want something badly enough, you can upgrade your skills in that area and accomplish your goals.

You are responsible for yourself!

Learning from Experience

You may say, "I just can't do it." "I just don't feel

like it." "After September 11, I've lost some gusto for life." The Talmud teaches us to always say, "This too is for good" (*Taanis* 21a) and "All the Merciful One does is for good" (*Berachos* 60b). These thoughts will help us to always learn positive lessons from every experience, even ones that seems negative.

The saying from *Mishlei* (24:16), "A righteous person falls seven times, and he keeps getting up," means that the righteous person keeps learning how to utilize his falling as a learning experience for the future.

In addition to the lesson quoted at the beginning of this chapter, the Mishnah in *Avos* 4:1 teaches three principles to achieve success: (1) rejoice with your portion, (2) learn from others, and (3) control and discipline yourself. Let us focus on applying these three steps in our lives:

1. Rejoice with your portion. Don't keep feeling sorry for yourself that you lack money, education, talent, the perfect job.... Believe that you are in the best situation for yourself now. Why? Because Hashem is in control and He has everything systematized in perfect order. Everything happens for a reason.

2. Learn from others. It is important to learn from others if you want to be able to grow. You can't expect to move forward in life if you don't add to your knowledge and your skills.

Hashem deliberately positions certain people in your life. One of the reasons for this is for you to learn from them to grow.

3. Control and discipline yourself. Take charge of your life. When you stop making excuses, you will make more progress. Pray more for Hashem's help, stop blaming other people, and begin making the improvements you know are necessary. It may not be easy, but your efforts will pay off.

Learning from Others

Try putting together a list of two or three happy people, two or three wise people, and two or three disciplined people that you know and admire. Start observing them more and try to learn their secrets to success. (If you don't know any such people personally, you can read biographies and learn about them that way.)

Prepare some questions that will help you grow and then approach the people on your list.

- "I think that I can use some help in _____. Can you give me some guidelines for success?"

- "I've noticed that you are very good at _____. Can you show me how it's done?"

- "Can you please spend a few minutes explaining to me how I can improve in this area?"

Keep learning and growing, trying different things when your current techniques don't seem to be good enough. Eventually you will find an even better situation, one which will be perfect for you at that stage of your growth.

If I am not for myself, who will be for me?
(*Avos* 1:14)

September 11 and you: On the first anniversary of September 11, there was significant media coverage of the many memorial ceremonies held. The next year, there was less coverage. Perhaps the news reporters felt that the people had already heard too much about 9/11 and there was nothing new to learn.

Learning is an ongoing event. We must constantly review what we have learned and put it into action. In addition, we can always rethink the past and keep learning from it.

Did something unusual or out of the ordinary happen to you today? Did something happen that made you stop and think?

What did you learn from these events? What should you have learned? Can you put these events into perspective in order to utilize them for future success?

Keep learning on all levels. Keep your eyes, ears, and mind open. Learning is an unending, inexhaustive process.

Chapter 7

The Big Question

About three thousand people went to work on September 11 thinking that they would be returning home that evening; yet they, their families, and the whole world were dealt with a shocking blow.

Pirkei Avos (2:15) states, "Repent the day before you die." This *mishnah* is worded in a strange way. Why does it say "the day before you die"? Why not "the day of your death — before it's too late?"

One of the lessons we learn from this is that we never know when that last day may be. We could miss the chance to do *teshuvah* (repentance) properly. Not only could we fail to do *teshuvah* on time, we could miss other opportunities as well, such as to complete or even to start some of our goals. Thus, we need to say, every single day, "If not now, when?" (*Avos* 1:14).

Think seriously about what it is that you really want to do with your life. How can you improve the quality of your life, beginning this very day? What do you excel at? What can you excel at? We need to learn to count our days, every day. "Teach us to count our days, so that we develop a heart of wisdom" (*Tehillim* 90:12).

Success on the Job

How can you excel in your endeavors? How can you join the top ten percent in your field?

Perhaps you have heard of the successful comedian who reads and writes some fifteen hundred jokes daily to use twenty of them for his evening show. This routine shows a commitment to succeed. Do you show the same type of commitment to succeed at your goals?

We need to commit ourselves to excelling in what we do. We need to overcome obstacles and push for growth.

Imagine this were your last day at your job. Ask yourself, "Can I do it right, to perfection?" Commit yourself, with Hashem's help, to doing your best for one day.

Here are some suggestions you may try to make this "last" day a success:

- Remove the "Do not disturb" sign (whether real or imaginary) from your cubicle area and post a new sign: "How can I help you?"

- Consider how you want your coworkers to remember you: Look around your work space and consider how you could brighten up your corner of the office. Remove some of the junk and any posters or slogans that could be offensive to some and ask yourself, "Is this what I really want to stand for?"

Love Your Work

Pirkei Avos (1:10) teaches us that Hashem wants us to love our work. We are also taught that a Jew's primary function is to serve Hashem through learning Torah and doing mitzvos, as the Mishnah teaches, "All your actions should be for the sake of Heaven" (*Avos* 2:17).

If your present job doesn't suit your goals in life, consider looking for one that gives you joy, satisfaction, and meaning. Then you can channel all of your energies into becoming better at what you do.

If this seems impossible, strive to excel at what you are doing and see whether you can develop a liking for it or modify it to your liking.

Some may be saying, "But I have to earn a living. I can't afford to experiment."

When will you be able to "experiment"? Are you waiting to win a million dollars in a lottery?

Well, the reality is that very few people win the lottery. Thus, you must, as best as you are able, set aside illusions of financial security and explore what you were placed on this earth to accomplish. It is a grave mistake to waste part of your life on a career that does not utilize your talents and maximize your potential.

The Talmud (*Berachos* 43b) teaches, "Hashem designed a certain profession to suit each person just right."

It seems too easy, doesn't it? If I like my work so much that it makes me happy, it doesn't seem quite right. Isn't work supposed to be work? There can be times when work seems like play, because you enjoy it so much. Is that really possible? Certainly you know of people who are working at a profession or job well beyond retirement age, even though they don't seem to be in need of the money. These people may love their work. They are not doing it for the money. This is what we should all strive for. Similarly, Torah study is described in terms of toil and labor, and it is also the greatest enjoyment.

Your Full Potential

I know a young man who, when he was twelve years old, reviewed one *mishnah* of *Maseches Berachos* (5:1, "One should not begin to say *Shemoneh Esrei* until he is in an appropriate state of mind") twenty thousand times. He may have achieved a world record or even a historical record of learning one *mishnah* the most times.

What is the purpose of such an exercise? Besides the reward for such Torah learning, which is incalculable, there is the great accomplishment of breaking loose from mental bonds that hold us back and chain us down.

You are probably capable of achieving far more than you have — as of yet.

Consider which is better for you: learning one hundred *mishnahyos* or one *mishnah* one hundred times?

It may be more difficult to learn the one *mishnah* a hundred times. Why? After learning it a few times, a person tends to think that he has covered the subject, that there is nothing more to be gained. Thus, it is a greater challenge to learn the *mishnah* a hundred times, with a view of seeing something that you didn't see before each time. Although this is not so easy for everyone, those who do it can learn to really appreciate how profound a single *mishnah* can be. They can then go on to learn one hundred *mishnayos* at a much higher level of understanding.

Ground Zero

The area where the Twin Towers once stood is referred to as "ground zero." We can look at this as a reminder to view each day as a new start on life.

There was a Jew who came upon an innovative idea to save his spiritual life. He was always busy. He worked morning, noon, and night and had hardly any time for Torah study. Then he forced himself to being studying Torah for an hour or two a day. Soon afterwards, his wife and others confronted him: "How can you neglect your business responsibilities like this?"

He replied: "What will happen when I die? I won't be working then, either. But then, there will be no alternative. So imagine that for this daily hour or two I'm dead."

This idea saved his spiritual life. This type of attitude represents a form of "spiritual ground zero," a state of mind exemplified by thinking that every day is a brand new gift from Hashem, which must be utilized in His service.

This type of zero-based thinking will help us make better choices in life. It is a key approach to changing our lives.

September 11 and you: Take a moment now to objectively review your accomplishments in life. If, after your review, you find that you are still on "ground zero," pray to Hashem that He give you the courage and strength to reach your goals. Now is a good time to build.

If, however, after your review, you find that you are quite a bit above ground zero, do not become complacent. The concept of "ground zero" is not limited to the ground. If a person is standing still in a figurative sense, he is not making progress. Life is a series of ladders. A ladder is made for going up or down; sitting or standing still isn't an option. So, look closer. If you are making progress in your goals, great! Consider whether you can do even better. If you are not making progress, look for ways to start moving again.

Chapter 8

The People Connection

What is the best approach for success in life?
(*Avos* 2:13)

Five different answers are given to this question. The two that we will focus on here are "good friends" and "good neighbors."

A person can choose to change himself completely, but if he continues to associate with his old group of friends he will end up back to the same habits, customs, and manners (*Mesilas Yesharim*, ch. 5).

We are influenced by the people we associate with. We adopt their attitudes, mannerisms, and even their dress code.

To make positive changes in our lives, we need to select a new social group. "Keep far away from bad neighbors and do not be friends with wicked people" (*Avos* 1:7). Work and socialize only with the kind of people you want your children to be like when they grow up.

Do Things with Others

Koheles (4:9) teaches that two are better than one. This advice works for all types of activities, from going shopping or taking a walk to building a business.

We also learn from the negative. The gang of terrorists who destroyed the Twin Towers and hijacked two other planes were not individuals working on their own. They were backed by an intricate network of evildoers who spent many years planning their deeds of mass destruction.

We can use this as a model for us in a positive way. We need to build networks of positive people to help us grow and build up the world. The Mishnah (*Sanhedrin* 71b) spells this out: "If the wicked are scattered, it is better for them and the world.... If they gather together, it is bad for them and for the world...." However, it is good for the righteous to gather together for they will produce more Torah and mitzvos, which protect them and the whole world.

"Who is honored? One who honors others" (*Avos* 4:1). If you show your friends respect, they will show you respect and they will tell others that you are a person who respects the rights of others. It's a beautiful circle, one that can grow even larger when we do it with the proper intent.

There is a mitzvah to join in with groups of righteous individuals: "With a multitude of people, it is a glory for the king" (*Mishlei* 14:28).

To get even more benefit from your associations, don't just join, become more involved. Look at the various committees that are available in your community. Find out which ones are the most active in bringing honor to Hashem and volunteer to serve on those committees. The people you will meet and befriend will be like-minded individuals who will help you grow in all areas of life.

The key to keep in mind is to respect others. Honor each person for his qualities. Try to help others get what they need, as well. The more you help others, the more Hashem will help you, measure for measure.

When Hashem created Adam, the first man, He said, "It is not good for man to be alone" (*Bereishis* 2:18). This verse is generally interpreted as referring to getting married. However, we can also apply it in a broader sense. We need the opinion and input of others in all matters. We are taught that Torah should be learned with a study partner for maximum benefit (see *Avos* 3:3). The Talmud (*Berachos* 63b) even teaches that there is a danger to studying alone when one can learn with others and that it also leads to foolishness.

When we spend time with positive people, we become energized, more creative, more enthusiastic, and happier. We help, support, and encourage each other. Each of us can accomplish more together than an individual can achieve alone.

Guard your friendships. Because they are so essential and productive, you must be careful to maintain them with positivity and high quality. *Lashon hara* (gossip) and all other forms of cruelty have to be completely outlawed in your network of friends as a start.

"More than anything you guard, guard your mind, for from it comes all the results of life" (*Mishlei* 4:23). You must always avoid negative people who may ruin your chances of accomplishing your full potential.

The Benefits of a Mentor

The Mishnah (*Avos* 1:6, 1:16) teaches, "Accept upon yourself a mentor."

The same phrase is written twice in the first chapter of *Avos*. Is this a misprint? Certainly not. As is often the case, repetition is used to stress the importance of a subject.

The right teachers can make all the difference in your "*shteiging*" (growth) in life. They can save you from countless mistakes and promote and accelerate your growth.

We need different mentors at various stages in life. The rebbe who taught you the *alef-beis* may not be the one to advise you on finishing and reviewing

Shas (the Talmud). It is also possible that one may have more than one mentor at a time, each serving specific purposes in which he is an expert.

It takes some work to get close to a mentor. Sometimes you need strategies and planning. One method to get close to a mentor is taught in *Avos* 1:4: "Let your house be a meeting place for Sages, attach yourself to the dust of their feet, and drink in their words with thirst."

A relationship has to be established and maintained. It takes time and patience. There needs to be ongoing communication. It takes an investment of your time, which will pay off in many ways.

> *September 11 and you:* We have spoken in this chapter of the benefits of associating with the right people and having strong friendships. Sometimes, as a result of a disagreement or a misunderstanding, a long-time friendship becomes broken, seemingly lost. Rather than patching things up, we say to ourselves, "I don't want to be the one to apologize" or "I like this person very much, but I am scared to approach him to make amends. I will wait for the right time."
>
> The swiftness with which the events of September 11 occurred should remind us that we may not be able to wait for the "right time." Mending broken fences and friendships takes

time. As soon as possible, look for opportunities to rekindle worthwhile friendships. Purim is a good time to try to rejuvenate a lost friendship through sending *mishloach manos* (gifts to friends). The *Yamim Nora'im* (the "Days of Awe," Rosh HaShanah and Yom Kippur) are also an opportune time, since everyone is seeking to repent and make amends. Every *erev Rosh Chodesh*, which is known as *Yom Kippur Katan* ("Small Yom Kippur"), can similarly be utilized to make a new start.

If you should be approached by a former friend to make amends, do not turn aside as if he is not there. Seek to rekindle the friendship and not to rekindle the feud. Making peace is a great mitzvah at all times and any time is a good time to say, "I'm sorry and let's be friends."

(For more on this topic, see our book *Be a Friend* [Southfield, MI: Targum Press, 2002].)

Chapter 9

Profound Thinking

O ne of the greatest benefits we all gained from the terrible disaster of the toppling of the Twin Towers is that it pressed us into thinking. Our thoughts are powerful. They can guide us to create incredible things. The "Twin Towers" in our minds can be greater than the ones in Manhattan. On the other hand, misguided thoughts can cause much damage. Therefore, it is of utmost importance that we seek to think in a manner that builds, rather than destroys.

The amazing brain is estimated at having about eighteen billion cells, each of which is connected to as many as twenty thousand others. We have the capacity to learn at an incredible rate and to retain tons of information. The Talmud (*Kesubos* 17a) teaches that when a Torah scholar passes away it is as if a *sefer Torah* (Torah scroll) has been removed from the world. We see from this that a person has the potential of a *sefer Torah*, filled with an unlimited amount of Hashem's wisdom.

"One who has [wisdom] has everything" (*Nedarim* 41a). You can become very wise by developing your mind. You can tap into your brain power and channel it to energize your life. Shlomo HaMelech says, "The length of days is in her right hand; in her left is wealth and honor" (*Mishlei* 3:16). This refers to the Torah, which guides us to prime the pump of wisdom in our mind and heart.

The first of the morning blessings thanks Hashem for the gift of a mind to understand the difference between day and night. The mind is capable of countless applications and uses. It is versatile, flexible, and portable. You have the ability to create a multimillion dollar industry and more with your mind. You carry your assets with you everywhere you go. What a great gift of kindness from Hashem!

We take the brain so much for granted that we do not even think about it, to the extent that we are deceived into thinking that it is not really all that much. In actuality, one should imagine his mind as the most sophisticated of computers that fills an entire city block. If you woke up one morning to find a million dollars in hundred-dollar bills stacked at your front door, it would still not be as significant as finding that your brain is functioning!

Of course, this great gift requires regular maintenance. In the *Shemoneh Esrei*, the first of the daily requests (following the three introductory blessings) is a request for brain power: "You graciously grant a person wisdom and teach man understanding. Grant us wisdom, understanding, and knowledge from You. Blessed are You, Hashem, gracious Giver of knowledge." This acknowledgment, which we make three times a day, should help us appreciate and utilize the greatest of gifts Hashem has bestowed upon us.

Developing Your Brain Power

You can develop and increase your reservoir of wisdom by engaging in Torah study, which sharpens the mind and trains it to think as Hashem thinks. This is why Torah study is the greatest of all mitzvos (*Peah* 1:1). Some people consider Torah study too difficult and put it off for something to do later, maybe when they're retired. *Pirkei Avos* (5:27) addresses this very challenge: "According to the difficulty is the reward." We must realize that Hashem sets up challenges for us and that He holds us accountable for how we react to them.

The more we use our mind in a positive, Torah way, the more we gain. One extra review can lead to tremendous results. There is no comparison between one who reviews his lesson one hundred times and one who reviews it one hundred and one times (*Chagigah* 9b). The extra review can lead to a significant breakthrough in understanding. A single insight can sometimes change a person's life.

There may be some skeptics who question this idea, who believe that the benefits of Torah study are limited, *chas veshalom* (God forbid). We all have heard of famous athletes who practiced long hours every day for years before they reached their goals. The same is true of great musicians, who practice for hours at a time. We don't have to limit our survey to athletes or musicians — look at doctors. The competition to enter medical school is intense and, if one is admitted, medical school is a long, tedious program. But it's worth it to those who choose that route.

Torah study, *lehavdil*, is the same. Some may think that Torah scholars have limited knowledge, that their expertise is limited to the religious sphere. The truth, however, is that the Talmud covers all areas of human endeavor. If you have ever conversed with a true Torah scholar, you know that his immense knowledge is not limited to the sectarian world. Torah scholars are experts in all areas of life. Torah study is the training ground for all aspects of life, but, *lehavdil*, like athletics, if you do not exercise every day you will not be up to the challenge.

The Secret to Wisdom

The Talmud (*Berachos* 4a) teaches that we should always train our tongue to say, "I don't know." It is a major mistake to conclude that we know all there is to know about a subject. A person with such an attitude can get stuck in his arrogance to the point where he cannot be helped. His mind is closed.

However, "a wise person is one who learns from every person" (see *Avos* 4:1). Imagine looking around at others and thinking, *I can learn valuable lessons from each of these individuals.* We need to train ourselves to say, "I don't know it all." We need to always be eager to learn more and grow wiser. "Drink in the words of [the Sages] with thirst" (*Avos* 1:4).

We have to always keep our minds open and keep saying: "I'm not sure." "I don't know." "I need to learn more on this subject."

The question, "Who is wise?" is posed in two places in the Talmud, and two different answers are given:

1. "One who learns from every person" (*Avos* 4:1).

2. "One who thinks ahead" (*Tamid* 32a).

Learning from others is how we gain new insights. We can think of ideas on our own, too, but two heads are better than one. We can think better when we are open to ideas from all others. But, in order to deal with the future, we need to also think ahead and anticipate it, to explore the contingencies. Thus, there are two keys to wisdom: learning from others and thinking ahead.

Before investing in a business deal, speak to others for their input and think it over carefully. By the same token, when you come up with a new idea or develop a product or service that is a little better, faster, or cheaper than what is already available, learn from others and think ahead in order to make it successful.

Asking Questions

We learn the key to developing one's mind from the system used at the Pesach seder. To start the discussion at the seder, we ask a series of four questions. This system of asking and answering opens up the mind. We have to be willing to consider options in dealing with a question or a problem. Ask first questions first (*Avos* 5:10). Use a logical order.

What exactly are you trying to accomplish? Is there a problem? What might be an ideal solution? Asking a question opens the mind and expands your thinking. You become more creative, curious, and eager to develop a viable solution.

Admit the Truth

Pirkei Avos (5:10) teaches that there are seven steps to true wisdom. One of these steps is "to admit the truth." A person must be willing to abandon an idea if it is proven to be incorrect. Admit that you are wrong. Always remain open to the possibility that you are fallible. Then you will always be willing to consider new ideas and insights.

We need to be flexible, ready and willing to change and try new approaches. If you are willing to learn new approaches, there are no limits to what you can achieve.

In the first blessing before the morning Shema, we say, "In His goodness, Hashem renews the work of creation every day, regularly." Rav Hutner, *zt"l*, explains that this serves as a model for us: Always renew your thinking. Consider things from scratch, modify, perfect, reconsider, and grow.

We need to look at each day not as if it is just another day but as if it were a new day, because it is one. Rashi, in commenting on the Shema (*Devarim* 6:6, "These words which I command you this day"), teaches that the Torah you learn daily should be as a new message, a message you just received from the Creator of the Universe.

The Daily Power-Message

We are instructed to recite the Shema at least twice daily (*Devarim* 6:7). But, of course, there is much more to the Shema than merely speed-reading it and then forgetting about it. We should concentrate on the words and then apply them at all times of the day.

The Shema contains three mitzvos that we can fulfill daily:

1. Apply the Torah to your heart, as it says, "These words which I command you today should be on your heart" (ibid., 6). This

means that a person should study Torah at least an hour a day with the objective of getting the information into his heart.

How should you accomplish this goal? Try the following: Learn with a *chavrusa* (study partner). Take good notes and review them. Reflect on what you are learning. Think about how you can apply the lessons you have learned to your daily life. Imagine yourself using the information at the next opportunity.

One who does not study Torah regularly is in serious danger of being controlled by the *yetzer hara* (the evil inclination). Furthermore, our Sages teach that if you learn more Torah, you will be successful in all areas of your life (*Tehillim* 1:2–3).

2. Learn Torah constantly, as it says, "You shall speak about [the Torah] while at home and on the road, at night and in the morning" (*Devarim* 6:7). Nowadays, this can be accomplished by listening to Torah tapes. Traveling time can be learning time. You can turn your travel time into a regular *seder* (fixed learning time) for learning or reviewing Chumash, Mishnah, *Tehillim*, or anything else.

3. Teach Torah, as it says, "You shall teach them to your children... " (ibid. 11:19). One of our goals in learning should be to always share

the lessons with others. When asked at the Shabbos table to give over a *d'var Torah* (a discussion on a Torah topic), many people respond, "I really don't know anything" or "I have nothing to say." You are a great person. You have much to teach. But how can others learn from you if you will not open your heart to prepare lessons to teach?

September 11 and you: We have been discussing the amazing entity called the brain. The terrorists who murdered thousands of innocent people on September 11, 2001, used their brains to carry out mass destruction. We, however, can use our brains to accomplish great goals, through Torah learning and mitzvah observance.

Hashem has given you a great brain. Use it!

Chapter 10

Challenges

Our brain is the tool that helps us to overcome every challenge we face. Challenges in life are part of the normal course of events. *Mesilas Yesharim* (chapter 1) teaches that "all matters of this world are tests to a person." They are a necessary part of life, for they trigger opportunities for us to make choices. You can choose to respond to a challenge in a positive and constructive manner and thus bring out your best qualities.

We were put in this world in order to come closer to Hashem. David HaMelech says: "One thing I have asked of Hashem...to dwell in the house of Hashem all the days of my life" (*Tehillim* 27:4). We must rise above our current surroundings, limitations, and problems, and imagine being closer to Hashem and soaring to the heights of perfection with His assistance.

How can we achieve this? As discussed in earlier chapters, we need clear goals, vivid mental pictures, and positive guidelines for ongoing growth. When we are determined, focused, and enthusiastic, and we pray to achieve a goal, Hashem will make it happen.

The wicked terrorists were able to accomplish their goals partly because of their intense emotional hatred, which stimulated them to a frightening degree of energy.

It says in *Tehillim* (118:1, 136:1, et al.), "Give thanks to Hashem for He is good, for His goodness endures forever." It is our job in this world to come closer to Hashem and to walk in His ways. We have a duty to emulate Hashem and pursue goodness. Thus, one of the greatest lessons for us to learn from September 11 is to become obsessed with goodness and kindness. By developing an obsession to do good, we impress our commitment onto our personality until it reaches our subconscious mind.

Obstacles

What makes it difficult for us to serve Hashem? The Talmud (*Berachos* 17b) provides the answer: "We desire to fulfill Your will, but what is blocking us? The yeast in the dough [i.e., our inner inclination, which we need to overcome and control], and the oppression of the nations [i.e., outside pressures]."

Which of these two is the primary obstacle? Based on the Mishnah in *Avos*, "Who is the mighty one? He who conquers his inclination" (*Avos* 4:1), we can say that the inner inclination, the *yetzer hara*, is the more difficult to overcome.

We need to keep asking ourselves the key question: "What in me is holding me back?"

A follow-up question is also important: "Is there a particular skill I need to develop? Is there a weakness I need to overcome? What can I do to correct the situation?"

As you dig inside, you will discover how to unlock your potential. As the Rambam (*Hilchos Sechirus* 13:13) explains, we need to apply "all of our strength" in fulfilling our obligations in life. This concept is not limited to our thinking strength. We may need to rethink our evaluation of our physical capabilities so that we can truly use all of our strength to accomplish our goals.

You may need proper instruction and practice, but there is a lot more you can do if you have the desire and determination.

Learn to Speak

Do you present yourself well? Are you articulate? Are you fluent in the language you speak?

You can learn to use words to develop your skills to a higher level. Hashem created man with two unique skills, intellect and speech, which are intertwined with each other. Each word is a tool to express a thought. With a better vocabulary, you can think better and form more complex ideas.

However, we are not speaking about a mere increase in the quantity of words at your disposal. The Talmud (*Pesachim* 2b) teaches how essential it is to minimize one's words and to always speak in a refined manner. That is, the more qualitative (descriptive, clear, and meaningful) your vocabulary is, the more you will be respected and listened to by others. Your language skills are key measures of your intelligence and ability to process information.

How does one attain this "qualitative" speech pattern? One method is preparation. When possible, try rehearsing what you will say in your mind before your words leave your lips. Try analyzing ideas from both sides. That is, try to see how your words could be misconstrued and then "rewrite" your thoughts before they are released.

You can also rehearse your thoughts or words with a good friend who can serve as an audience and a critic, as well. Or write down your thoughts beforehand and then edit your speech. Another alternative is to take a speaking or writing course from an expert who can guide and coach you.

It is also very important to engage in a daily study of the *sefer Chafetz Chaim*, which teaches how to avoid negative speech and to communicate effectively.

Your Intuition

The Talmud (*Niddah* 45b) says that women have

"an extra measure of *binah* (understanding)." They can sense the rightness of a course of action or situation, judge people more accurately, and develop certain types of ideas better.

All of us can develop the skill of listening to our inner voice better in order to achieve more and greater accomplishments. How can this be done?

We have all heard our "inner voice" speak to us in the past: "Should you really be doing this?" "Don't you have more important things to do?" "When will you reach the level of your forefathers?" We must not only hear our "inner voice," we must also stop and pay attention to it, act upon it, and let it speak louder.

As we discussed previously, the Mishnah in *Avos* (4:1) teaches that the secret to wisdom is to learn from every person. Another facet of the *mishnah* is to also learn from yourself, since you are included in the category "every person."

You can actually change your life by asking yourself questions and listening to the answers. Try taking a blank sheet of paper and writing out your current goals or problems as a question. For example, "How can I improve my relationship with my children?" Write down at least ten different answers to that question. This will unlock your thinking power and you will generate many ideas, with Hashem's help.

After you have at least ten methods of improving your relationships on your list, select one that you can act on immediately. Now repeat this process by asking yourself for ten ideas of how to implement this method. "With plans you prepare yourself and with strategies you go to battle" (*Mishlei* 20:18).

Ideas can energize you when you look for them and invite them into your thoughts. They can uplift you, excite you, and enlighten you.

Seeking Help from Hashem

The story is told of someone who kept a journal of challenges that came his way for about ten years. Each time he had a problem he would record the possible solutions. Then, when the problem was resolved, he would note how things had actually worked out. Incredibly, in most cases, Hashem sent solutions that he had not even anticipated.

This shows us that there are always options for dealing with situations and that Hashem is in control. He tests us, sees how we respond, and helps us achieve our goals.

When you use all of your abilities, wholeheartedly, at the highest level, Hashem will prosper your efforts in incredible ways. Begin with greater efforts in your prayers and in evaluating yourself with more respect for your unique potential.

You may be thinking, *Who says I deserve Hashem's help? I may not be worthy of His attention.*

The answer to this is that no one is completely worthy, but Hashem promises to assist us when we turn to Him for help. For example, see *Tehillim* (81:11): "Open your mouth wide, and I will fill it." As we succeed, we must keep praying and acknowledging that "it is He who gives you the capability to acquire wealth" (*Devarim* 8:18 and *Targum*).

How can you justify deserving more than the average person?

When you dedicate yourself to serving Hashem, you justify your existence. When you devote yourself to emulating the ways of Hashem, for example by doing acts of kindness like He does (see *Michah* 7:18), you will merit special assistance.

You have special talents, given to you by Hashem, who is waiting for you to utilize them so that He can assist you in amazing ways.

September 11 and you: After September 11, 2001, the United States Congress passed much legislation. A new cabinet position was created, called "Home Land Security." This legislation attempted to provide law enforcement personnel with "legal weapons" to wage war in the new battlefront of "The War against Terrorism."

A war is a battle for survival. A war tests a nation's determination to survive. We, as individuals, are also engaged in a war of a similar nature. We have to constantly wage battles within ourselves to determine how we are going to use our time and our resources. This battle, our Sages say, is called "the great battle of life" (*Chovos HaLevavos* 5:5).

Each of us was placed upon this earth to accomplish great achievements. We are unique individuals. However, we must be aware that the *yetzer hara* seeks to do battle with us each day. Therefore, we must make a conscious choice as to who is going to win and the strategies we should employ to win the war.

Have you committed yourself to a fixed time for Torah study on a daily basis? If not, what is your strategy? "If not now, when?" (*Avos* 1:14).

Do you perform mitzvos with joy? If not, what is your strategy? "If I am only for myself, what am I?" (ibid.).

Have you evaluated how you use your time? Can you rearrange your time so that you can make a more concerted effort to wage a battle against the *yetzer hara*, which seeks to take away your time and deprive you of spiritual growth?

Have you evaluated how you spend your resources? Do you spend too much money on luxuries? Do you have a strategy for reallocating your resources so that you focus on the big picture?

Have you asked the Chief Commander for assistance on all battlefronts? If you have not, as of yet, been successful, have you re-approached the Chief to plead again for more resources, more ideas, more patience, more kindness, and the courage to strive to succeed?

We wish and pray for your success in this great battle. "Hope to Hashem, strengthen yourself and He will give you courage" (*Tehillim* 27:14) — to win all of your battles!

Chapter 11

The Hidden Benefits

We are taught to accustom ourselves to live by the principle set forth in the Gemara (*Taanis* 21a): "This too is for good" (*gam zu letovah*). Every problem has within it the potential to be turned into a great success story. Using this approach, the events of the Twin Towers tragedy, which leave us stunned and bewildered, will some day be looked upon as a trigger of the greatest of benefits.

Certainly, the events of September 11 have far-reaching historical effects. We need to internalize the concept of *gam zu letovah* until we can respond with it automatically whenever a difficulty arises.

In order to reach this level, we need to first develop the general understanding that everything in this world is good (*Bereishis* 1:31) and that "all that the Merciful One does is for good" (*Berachos* 60b). We have to overcome our self-limiting beliefs, which tend to belittle the goodness all around us.

There are many events and situations that you

encounter on a daily basis that are not under your control. However, how you relate to and interpret them is under your control. You can choose to connect more to the teachings of the Torah. Put a positive spin on these events that occur and you will be surprised to see how positively things turn out. When the glass is half full, why focus on the part that seems empty? Always see the positive in everything that happens. Keep saying, "It's good" or "It's great, *baruch Hashem!*"

Every difficulty is actually good because it helps you grow. We have to train ourselves to keep responding with "it's good" and then to focus on discovering how and why the situation is actually good.

Change the word *problem* to *test, challenge, opportunity*, or *gift*, and you will be more positive and ready to deal with it in a constructive manner.

Training Program

Our Sages say, "Train yourself to always say, 'All that the Merciful One does is for good' " (*Berachos* 60b). We need to prepare ourselves for every eventuality. Just as athletes continually prepare for competition, you can prepare yourself for the "competition" of life by writing down the above phrase on a card that you can carry with you and review regularly. (You can also write to us at P.O. Box 82, Staten Island, NY, 10309 for some free printed cards that are available.) A person can choose to think about his limitations or about his potential. There is a tremendous difference. The choice is yours.

Timing

Included in the understanding that "everything is good" is the lesson of timing. Every goal takes a certain amount of time to materialize. You need patience and the awareness that Hashem knows just the right time to help you. Relax and trust in Hashem that He is caring for you.

Every time you fall, Hashem picks you up. At the same time, He is also the One who pushed you down, and He did so for a beneficial purpose. Look for the good. When you fall down, always pick something up.

I know of a family whose home was discovered to have termites. They were told that some of the walls needed to be taken apart in order to be repaired. The construction people suggested that the owners could rearrange some of their rooms as part of the process. Thus, taking down some of the walls had an unexpected, beneficial result: more space.

Look for the lessons in every event that occurs. Respond in a creative, positive, and constructive way. You will find some good when you realize that it is definitely there.

September 11 and you: Related to the concept

of positive thinking is overcoming one's reluctance to move ahead. Some might think that it is no use to go forward, to build anew, because terrorists may destroy it in the end, *chas veshalom*.

We do not know the whole picture. We cannot know what lies ahead. However, we must always think positive and plan for the future in spite of the events of September 11. We must not let the events of 9/11 hold us back. On the contrary, we must do everything possible to counteract the acts of tremendous evil. We must awaken within ourselves the power to rise up against difficulties and build anew.

When we recall September 11, are our thoughts directed to the destruction or to the need to rebuild? Are our thoughts directed to the lack of mercy of the terrorists or to the emergency personnel and others who saved their fellow human beings?

Baruch Hashem, we have much to be thankful for. We need to view the events from the right perspective.

Chapter 12

Dealing with Disappointments

The downing of the Twin Towers is a tragic disappointment. Should we compound it now by blowing up, being angry, and blaming others?

On a personal level, on a day-to-day basis, how should we respond?

We need to recover and continue forward with more drive than ever. We need to think ahead more, to anticipate what may go wrong. We need to take precautions to guard against setbacks and problems. We need to know that disappointments are part of Hashem's program for us in life.

> *A person is tested in three ways: by his purse, by his anger, and by his drinking.*
>
> (Eiruvin 65b)

In the case of the Twin Towers, the first two elements are clearly present: there were great financial losses and there is anger. Hashem is testing us to see how we will react.

"Who is wise? One who sees that which will develop" (*Tamid* 32a). This principle is applicable in every person's daily life. You can prepare for dealing with disappointments in advance.

There is a Torah premise that when we decide to accomplish anything worthwhile in life, we are going to face all types of challenges and difficulties. Obstacles are tests to see if we will become discouraged.

When we anticipate possibilities in advance, we can respond quickly and effectively, when necessary. There will be fewer surprises to throw us off balance. You can say, "I know what this setback is all about. I will not let it get me down. I will be unstoppable, with Hashem's help."

Almost every parashah of the Torah has examples of shock waves that people had to deal with:

- *Parashas Bereishis* — Adam and Chavah ate from the Tree of Knowledge against Hashem's wishes and were punished with death, hard labor, and difficulty in childbearing, as well as expulsion from Gan Eden. The Talmud (*Eiruvin* 18b) teaches that in response to these punishments Adam spent 130 years repenting for this sin.

- *Parashas Noach* — Noach and his family were the sole survivors of the great flood. Noach then brought sacrifices from all the pure animals out of gratitude for being saved.

- *Parashas Lech Lecha* — Avraham left his home as a result of Hashem's command and then had to leave Eretz Yisrael because of famine, yet he went willingly without complaining.

- *Parashas Vayeira* — A rainstorm of fire and sulfur destroyed the cities of Sedom and Amorah, and Lot and his two daughters were the only survivors. Yet Lot's daughters involved themselves in having children, hoping to rebuild the world. This eventually led to the birth of Rus, ancestress of Mashiach.

- *Parashas Chayei Sarah* — Sarah died when she heard that her only son, Yitzchok, was nearly offered as a sacrifice. After burying her, Avraham continued his great career of serving Hashem joyfully and wholeheartedly.

We need to contemplate these examples from the Torah and others throughout Tanach and *Shas* and learn from them how to react to difficulties and disappointments.

Take a minute to think about what you could do if you needed to look for another job. It pays to think in advance, "What could my next job be?" Although we should not necessarily spend an inordinate amount of time considering such things, thinking ahead to a certain degree is a mitzvah and a form of wisdom. It also helps us to stay focused and appreciative.

My father, *shlita*, was a furrier for many years. When things were shifting in that industry, he needed to find a new trade. He ended up making plastic slip-covers, which was similar to the work he had been doing. Instead of cutting and fitting furs, he was cutting and fitting plastic.

Hashem created us with the ability to adapt and to learn new skills. We have to think ahead and anticipate changes and even expect the unexpected.

Hashem gave us the ability to think through possible eventualities and to plan methods for dealing with them. For example, it is a mitzvah for a person to develop a regular savings plan in order to build a cash reserve for emergencies (see *Bava Metzia* 42a with *Rashi*). How does one get started on such a savings plan? One needs to discipline himself to live within his income limits and to avoid debts. It is helpful to have a monthly budget with a certain amount set aside for savings.

Mishlei (28:14) teaches: "Fortunate is a person who is always afraid."

The Talmud (*Gittin* 57b) explains that constantly being afraid of angering Hashem is beneficial, since it keeps a person from doing foolish, reckless things. We need to consider preparing and developing certain skills and abilities.

It's time for all of us to think: What did we do right on September 11? What should we do differently if, *chas veshalom*, something like that ever happened again?

Focusing on improvement helps us stimulate our creativity.

> *September 11 and you:* In the summer of 2003, there was a power failure in the northeast portion of the United States, Ohio, and Canada. About fifty million people were without power for a while. Some were concerned that the blackout was caused by terrorists, but it was shortly determined that the problem was technical and not actually terrorist related.
>
> It was reported that the people in New York who experienced the power outage were not as upset as they might have been before September 11. They realized that it was, in comparison, a relatively minor problem.
>
> In this chapter, we have been discussing the benefits of "seeing" into the future to be prepared for dealing with disappointments. It is just as important to compare the present with

the past in order to evaluate what is important and what is not.

Review recent disappointments in your life and determine where they fit into the big picture: Is this a 9/11 event (a terrible tragedy) or an electrical blackout (something difficult but easier to deal with)?

Our response to any given situation should correspond to the stimulus.

Chapter 13

Six Questions

One of the difficult questions that arises from September 11 is, why did Hashem allow innocent people to perish at the hands of wicked people? This question can be approached from many angles, but one of the most fundamental lessons is that Hashem, in His great mercy, wants to shock us and to alert us to the purpose of life.

We are in this world to prepare for *Olam HaBa*, the World to Come (*Avos* 4:21).

The Talmud (*Shabbos* 31a) teaches that we will be asked six questions when we reach the next world (after 120 years). These six questions summarize all that Hashem expects us to accomplish in this world.

These are the six questions:

1. Did you act honestly in your business dealings?

2. Did you have a regular, set time to study Torah?

3. Did you try to raise a family?

4. Did you hope for Hashem's salvation?

5. Did you study Torah in depth?

6. Did you try to go even deeper in studying Torah?

How are these questions related to each other? The first and third questions concern dealings with people, while the other four concern connecting with Hashem. But what is the overall goal of all of them? *Mesilas Yesharim* (ch. 1) teaches that "a person was created to have pleasure with Hashem." This is our ultimate aim. By striving to deal with others honestly, learn Torah, raise a family, yearn for the redemption, and spend more time on our Torah learning, we are in essence living with Hashem, the greatest happiness.

The first of the six questions, successful and honest business relationships, sets the tone for all of the others. Integrity is the essential basis for every interaction we have in life. Integrity and honesty lead to sincerity, persistence, courage, and generosity. These join together to form a full picture of personal fulfillment and happiness. How so? The Sages teach that truth is Hashem's "signature" (*Shabbos* 55a). Thus, a person who is honest will endure in his ways and develop to emulate Hashem in all areas.

The second question, learning Torah, is equally

crucial, since Torah learning is equivalent to all of the other mitzvos (*Shabbos* 127a; *Peah* 1:1). What steps are you taking to increase your Torah knowledge? Have you considered learning the entire *Shas* (all six orders of the Mishnah)? If you already have done it once, are you working on repeating this great feat? Do you set aside a daily program to learn Torah? Do you have a learning partner? Have you acquired tapes or *sefarim* (books) for your Torah library? "If not now, when?" (*Avos* 1:14). [For practical learning suggestions and samples of these ideas, please contact us at P.O. Box 82, Staten Island, New York 10309, or at our website www.IloveHashem.com.]

The post-9/11 period is an eye-opener. September 11 changed and transformed us. Life in this world is over for the nearly three thousand people who died on that day, and life began anew for the many who nearly died that day. Do we value our life properly?

This leads us to the third question, "Did you try to raise a family?" By raising a family, we grant life to other precious souls, with Hashem's help.

Torah values set the tone for what we live for and how we live. Our values and priorities determine how we live and enjoy life. Those who live consistently with these values will be far happier than those who live merely for their careers or other secular values.

The fourth question, "Did you hope for Hashem's

salvation?" brings us to the realization that Hashem is in control. We must trust in Him and keep praying for His help.

The fifth and sixth questions take us back to Torah study. Why is there such a great emphasis on Torah study? The Torah is so deep that each verse of the Chumash contains 600,000 insights (*Shemiras HaLashon, Shaar HaTorah* 1)! "Everything is in Torah" (*Avos* 5:24). There is no end to what we can learn when it comes to Torah. We must open our hearts and minds to its depth.

Keeping in mind these six all-compassing questions will help us prepare for the next world.

The Importance of Honesty

Let us return to discussing honesty on a practical level. When it comes to this mitzvah, the Torah uses an expression we don't find elsewhere in the Torah: "Stay *far away* from falsehood" (*Shemos* 23:7). We have to always strive to be truthful, straightforward, and honest with everyone, as much as possible within halachic guidelines.

Honesty includes doing your work with competence, upgrading your skills continually, and keeping up with the advances in your industry or field.

Honesty means to always contribute fairly to your company and to your customers.

Honesty means not to expect to get more out of something than what you put in.

Honesty in Interpersonal Relationships

Honesty is important not just in business dealings but also in dealings with other people. The first question of the Talmud in *Shabbos* quoted at the beginning of this chapter can be interpreted, "Did you act honestly in your social dealings?" For example, if you wrong another person it is a good idea to admit your mistake and apologize. Being honest in such a case increases the trust between you and the other person.

Honesty works in a *middah keneged middah* (measure for measure) fashion. If you treat people with love, they will do everything they can to be honest with you in order not to hurt you. On the other hand, if someone is honest with you and you respond with verbal abuse: "How could you be so stupid?" "What made you think you could do that?" "Who do you think you are?" it will be very difficult for the other person to draw close to you and establish a true friendship.

The sense of honesty and the habit of truthfulness are two of the most important qualities we need to learn, practice, and teach our children.

September 11 and you: For many, September 11 created a dividing line. As the days, months, and years separate us from 9/11, we must make a decision: Is the line still there or is it fading in the past, soon to be invisible? Are we going to continue developing ourselves based on 9/11 or will we forget all about it?

September 11 can serve as a division in time that you can use to institute positive changes in attitude.

To begin a career of sincere honesty, act in a manner that causes others to want to act honestly with you and in a manner that does not cause the tower of your friendship to come tumbling down.

Chapter 14

Moving Forward

*One who comes to purify himself will be assisted
[from Heaven].*
(*Shabbos* 104a)

We have to get started towards our goals right away. As soon as we get into motion, Hashem causes opportunities to open up all around us.

Many people who achieve great things in life do so in areas completely different from the field in which they started. *Chovos HaLevavos* (*Shaar HaBitachon*) explains that Hashem arranges life this way to teach us that He is always in complete control.

Thus, we need to:

1. Dream bigger. We need to set bigger goals. "Open your mouth wide, and I will fill it" (*Tehillim* 81:11). A challenging, exciting, worthwhile goal can be achieved with Hashem's help, but you have to take the initiative. For example, we now have published

thirteen of these books, and we would, *b'ezras Hashem* (with Hashem's help), like to write even more, maybe even a hundred. But at one time there were none. In order to begin the journey, you have to start and you must continue to dream — dream big. "On the path one is determined to go he will be led" (*Makos* 10b).

2. Use all our strength. "There are four things that require *chizuk* — Torah, good deeds, prayer, and pursuit of livelihood" (*Berachos* 32b). Rashi explains that "*chizuk*" here means "constantly, with all of your strength." We need to throw ourselves wholeheartedly into whatever we decide to do.

   Get fully into it! Don't be afraid to commit yourself totally to the right causes.

3. Break loose. To move ahead, we may need to break loose from the chains that are holding us down. Avraham Avinu was instructed by Hashem, "*lech lecha*" (*Bereishis* 12:1) — to move away from his hometown to his future career of greatness.

4. Use your time wisely. It is essential that we use our time for good, since it is a limited, essential, and most precious resource. Time cannot be saved. It has to be invested, not wasted. When you invest it wisely, you gain the greatest returns on your investment in the future.

"Teach us to count our days," we ask Hashem, "so that we develop a heart of wisdom" (*Tehillim* 90:12).

The way you choose to use your time makes all the difference in the quality of your life today and in the future. "Minimize your other involvements and be involved in Torah" (*Avos* 4:12). Torah and mitzvos are the best use of your time and your energy.

To get the most done with the greatest results, you need to resist the temptation to clear up small, easy things first. Train yourself to focus your energy on the activities that are most important and valuable. Keep in mind that to "win" we need to consider "**W**hat's **I**mportant **N**ow?"

Ask yourself: "What would I being doing now if I had been in the Twin Towers when they collapsed, but somehow made it out alive? How would I change my life? What would I not get into or not start if I could do it over?"

Fortunately, we did not all experience the events of September 11 near ground zero. Nevertheless, we can use the events of 9/11 to begin anew in all areas of our lives. We must make a conscious decision to change, to move ahead, to dream big, and to ask Hashem regularly for help.

> *September 11 and you:* We do not know to what extent the terrorists wanted to cause damage, but Hashem is surely the controller of

all. Could they have foreseen all that has happened since then? Nearly three years later, the United States has been engaged in two wars; numerous laws were passed; a new agency was created; and a new word was added to everyone's vocabulary, *9/11*.

Nineteen men in four airplanes brought about these tremendous upheavals. But we must remain cognizant that Hashem was behind everything, and for good reason: "God caused it so that we should fear Him" (*Koheles* 3:14).

Conclusion

Give thanks to Hashem for He is good.
(*Tehillim* 118:1, 136:1)

We are obligated to emulate Hashem and to counteract acts of tremendous evil with acts of tremendous goodness.
What can you do to:

- increase your *chesed* level?

- show that you love Hashem?

- show that you love people?

- lower your anger level and increase your patience level?

- set aside more time to learn Torah?

- reach your life goals?

- improve your communication skills with the Master of the Universe?

Now is the time. You are responsible (see *Avos* 1:14).

We can take steps to protect ourselves from a tragedy like September 11. You might be saying, "Wait a minute. Isn't that the government's job?" We are not talking about military responses. One of the obvious steps that we should all be taking is to say the daily evening prayer against terrorists with more concentration. Right after Shema, in *maariv*, we say, "Please protect us and remove from us enemies, plague, famine, and sword...." This is one of the major actions Hashem wants and expects of us: Prayer. By praying to Hashem, we acknowledge that it is Hashem, and Hashem alone, who controls the world and that only He can save us.

May we all merit the Redemption speedily in our time.

Small Books.

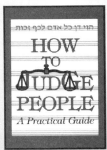

TARGUM PRESS Books

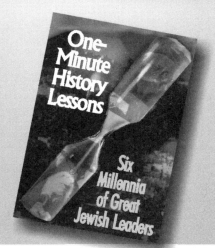